BROTHERTON POETRY PRIZE ANTHOLOGY III

Brotherton Poetry Prize Anthology III

2025

PRESENTED BY THE

UNIVERSITY OF LEEDS

POETRY CENTRE

judged by
SIMON ARMITAGE, MALIKA BOOKER,
KIMBERLY CAMPANELLO, ZAFFAR KUNIAL,
CAITLIN STOBIE, AND JOHN WHALE

with an introduction by
SIMON ARMITAGE

CARCANET POETRY

First published in Great Britain in 2025 by
Carcanet
Main Library, The University of Manchester
Oxford Road, Manchester, M13 9PP
www.carcanet.co.uk

A CIP catalogue record for this book is
available from the British Library.

ISBN 978 1 80017 519 8

Book design by Andrew Latimer, Carcanet
Typesetting by LiteBook Prepress Services
Printed in Great Britain by SRP Ltd, Exeter, Devon

The publisher acknowledges financial
assistance from Arts Council England.

CONTENTS

THE BROTHERTON PRIZE
PRESENTED BY THE UNIVERSITY OF LEEDS
POETRY CENTRE

The University of Leeds has a proud tradition of supporting new poetry and of exploring the poetry of the past. Geoffrey Hill was a member of staff from 1954 to 1978 and Leeds alumni include Jon Silkin, Ken Smith, Tony Harrison, Jeffrey Wainwright, Ian Duhig, and Linda France. The Poet Laureate Simon Armitage is Professor of Poetry. The University was ground-breaking in its inauguration of Gregory Fellows in the 1950s and among these the poets were James Kirkup, John Heath-Stubbs, Thomas Blackburn, Jon Silkin, William Price Turner, Peter Redgrove, David Wright, Martin Bell, Pearse Hutchinson, Wayne Brown, Kevin Crossley-Holland, and Paul Mills. The office of the international quarterly magazine *Stand* is located on campus. As a result, the poetry archives in the Brotherton Library are among the most extensive and valuable in the UK. More recently, the Academy of Cultural Fellows has included Douglas Caster Fellows Helen Mort, Malika Booker, Anthony Vahni Capildeo, Zaffar Kunial, and Matt Howard. The Leeds University Poetry Centre offers a dynamic resource for research, teaching, and public engagement by supporting and advancing the study of poetry both within and outside the University. It provides a focus for collaborative, interdisciplinary and individual research as well as offering a point of contact for the wider community to share in a range of activities, including readings, workshops, lectures and exhibitions.

The Poetry Centre works closely with the Brotherton Library whose literary collections are of international distinction. All four seventeenth-century Shakespeare folios sit alongside first editions and archival material relating to some of our most celebrated authors and playwrights including Ben Jonson, Charlotte and Emily Brontë and their brother Branwell, Elizabeth Gaskell, Charles Dickens, Evelyn Waugh and others. Our collections relating to living authors are outstanding and include the archive of our Professor of Poetry Simon Armitage. The Brotherton's reputation as a major research library is underpinned by the financial endowments left by its founder, Edward Allen Brotherton, 1st Baron Brotherton (1856-1930). The Library continues to enjoy a close relationship with the Brotherton family and we were delighted when the trustees of the Charles Brotherton Trust agreed to support a prize to encourage talented poets who have yet to publish a complete collection. This financial support has enabled the publication of this anthology. We are hugely grateful.

The winner of the 2019 Brotherton Poetry Prize was **Dane Holt**.

The winner of the 2021 Brotherton Prize was **Lauren Pope**.

The University of Leeds Poetry Centre acknowledges the assistance of our student intern Jon Gilbert and our Manager Matt Howard.

Dillon Jaxx is a queer non-binary writer disabled through chronic illness. Growing up trilingual sparked a passion for language and wordplay. Dillon's work explores the aftermath of trauma, illness, and addiction as well as the meaning of home, family, and identity. Their work has appeared in various publications online and in print, including *Poetry Wales*, *Alchemy Spoon*, and *Magma* and is currently displayed on various buses in Brighton. Dillon has been shortlisted and placed in numerous competitions and won the 2022 Rebecca Swift Prize 2022, the Wolverhampton Poetry Competition 2024, and the Live Canon International Poetry Competition in 2025. Their debut collection will be published in 2026.

NB: A version of *The Bodies in the Fridges at Work* was first published online by Nine Arches as part of the Nine Arches Primers series volume 6 shortlist 2021.

SHORTLISTED POETS

Will Fleming is a poet and Teaching Fellow in the School of English at Trinity College Dublin. He received his PhD from University College London in 2023, completing a thesis on contemporary Irish poetry and economics. His poetry has appeared or is forthcoming in *Gorse*, *Still Point*, *PDF*, *The Stinging Fly*, *The Stony Thursday Book*, and elsewhere. He was born in Limerick and is currently based in Dublin.

Lucy Holme is a writer and mother who lives in Cork, Ireland. Her poems feature in *PN Review*, *Poetry Ireland*,

Poetry London, *The London Magazine*, *Banshee*, *The Stinging Fly*, *Southword*, and *Poetry Wales*, amongst others. She has been shortlisted or runner up for The London Magazine Poetry Prize, The Red Line Poetry Competition, The Mairtín Crawford Award, The Wales Poetry Prize, and The Fool for Poetry Chapbook Award, and won the Cúirt New Writing Prize for Poetry and the Southword Editor's Prize 2024. Her debut chapbook, *Temporary Stasis* (shortlisted for The Patrick Kavanagh Award) was published by Broken Sleep Books in 2022. A nonfiction collection entitled *Blue Diagonals* was published by Broken Sleep Books in September 2024. She holds an MA with distinction in Creative Writing from UCC where she is currently studying for a PhD in Poetry.

Jam Kraprayoon is a Bangkok native who spends time there and in Washington, DC. He received a master's from Oxford and a bachelor's from the LSE and now works on AI policy. His work has been featured in *Poetry Wales*, *Beloit Poetry Journal*, *Portland Review*, and *Oxford Poetry*.

Adam Panichi (he/him) is a queer poet based between Italy and Leeds, where he works as a social worker. His poems have been published widely in journals including *And Other Poems*, *berlin lit*, *Strix*, *fourteen poems* and *Magma*. He was a runner-up in the Ledbury prize and his debut pamphlet *Cupid, Grown* will be published by Broken Sleep Books in 2025.

JUDGES OF THE BROTHERTON POETRY PRIZE FOR 2023

Simon Armitage was elected Oxford Professor of Poetry from 2015–2019, and in May 2019 was appointed UK Poet Laureate. He has published over a dozen collections, most recently *The Unaccompanied* (Faber, 2017) and *Blossomise* (Faber, 2024). His medieval translations include *Sir Gawain and the Green Knight* and *Pearl* which won the 2017 PEN Award for Poetry in Translation. He is a broadcaster, playwright, novelist and the author of three best-selling volumes of non-fiction. Simon was made CBE for Services to Poetry in 2015 and in 2018 was awarded the Queen's Gold Medal for Poetry. He is Professor of Poetry at the University of Leeds.

Malika Booker is a British Caribbean poet. Her poetry collection *Pepper Seed* (Peepal Tree Press, 2013) was longlisted for the OCM Bocas prize and shortlisted for the Seamus Heaney Centre prize (2014). She is published in *The Penguin Modern Poet Series 3 :Your Family: Your Body* (2017*)*. Malika was the Douglas Caster Cultural Fellow at University of Leeds and is currently a poetry Lecturer at Manchester Metropolitan University.

Kimberly Campanello is the author of the poetry-object and durational performance *MOTHERBABYHOME* (zimZalla, 2019). This year Bloomsbury Poetry will publish her collection *An Interesting Detail*. She is Professor of Poetry at the University of Leeds.

Zaffar Kunial was born in Birmingham and lives in Hebden Bridge. He published a pamphlet in the Faber New Poets series in 2014 and spent that year as the Wordsworth Trust Poet-in-Residence. He has spoken at numerous literary festivals and in programmes for BBC radio. He won the Geoffrey Dearmer Prize for his poem 'The Word'. His debut collection, *Us*, was published in 2019. His second full collection, *England's Green*, was published in 2023.

Caitlin Stobie is an author of fiction, poetry, and literary criticism. Her writing has won the Douglas Livingstone Creative Writing Competition, the Heather Drummond Memorial Prize for Poetry, and an Authors' Foundation Award. Her debut poetry collection, *Thin Slices*, was shortlisted for the Ingrid Jonker Prize for Poetry in 2024. She is a Lecturer in Creative Writing at the University of Leeds.

John Whale is the Director of the University of Leeds Poetry Centre. He is the author of two collections of poetry, *Waterloo Teeth* and *Frieze*, both published by Carcanet/Northern House. *Waterloo Teeth* was shortlisted for the Forward Prize's Felix Dennis Prize for best first collection. He is editor of the international quarterly magazine *Stand*.

INTRODUCTION
by Simon Armitage

If you're reading this, hello. Not everybody reads poetry – if they did, it wouldn't be poetry! This anthology contains the winning and shortlisted poems from The Brotherton Poetry Prize, a short manuscript competition organised by the University of Leeds Poetry Centre. Submissions of up to five poems are invited from poets who are yet to publish their first full-length book. It demands a level of consistency not required by single-poem prizes, but attracts entries from writers whose work is still developing or whose poems are yet to be fully appreciated. The Brotherton Prize is distinct in offering a kind of bridge or stepping stone towards something we call a collection, but as the following pages demonstrate, there is nothing provisional or incipient about the poems. For all they appear in sampler form here and as sections in an anthology, they are eminently publishable, and have been assessed by those standards, members of the judging panel acting as editors to some extent. As one of those judges I look for challenges and rewards within the language, for playfulness and poignancy, and for ideas being articulated in ways that are fresh and surprising — patterns and arrangements of words that I haven't heard before and wouldn't have thought of myself. I'm also looking for things I didn't know I was looking for, like "saunas heated by goodwill generated out of bitcoin mining" in *of people born unfree* by Will Fleming, or "The Polaroids and cheap plastic mascots, those flea market pendants, gilt peeling to reveal a hard interior, all your good intentions re-apportioned" in

(You were) decluttering before Marie Kondo made it famous by Lucy Holme, or "the congregation mumbling prayers/ as though they are ingredients for a meal / in a language they never plan to serve" in 'distended family' by Dillon Jaxx, or "*Fall webworms*, which eat the tender leaves/but avoid the larger veins and midrib / shrouding their meal in a silken mist" in 'An Inventory of Invasive Species' by Jam Kraprayoon, or a razor moving "as if peeling a film of air / from a pressed / flower" in 'Snow' by Adam Panichi. The winning and shortlisted poets receive a financial reward, but the bigger prize, I believe, is seeing their work in print, and by such an esteemed poetry publisher as Carcanet.

Poetry isn't for everybody. It is sometimes described as a well kept secret. If you're reading this I guess the cat is out of the bag.

BROTHERTON POETRY PRIZE ANTHOLOGY III

FOR WILL FLEMING

OUR REVENGE WILL BE THE LAUGHTER OF OUR CHILDREN

in memory of John Killer

a lot of slides on method
a glimpse of hotel women
voiced by Daphne
                    and in English
even though i'm not a poet
the blunt leaden-tipped arrow nevertheless
        comes to sprout
here: poetry is weather
                the weather it configures
a Derridean, necessarily rebarbative
hedgehog
                    painting in the post-Derridean ballpit
materialities of poetic language as continuous
with entities
oil   is mid
         is tradition
         air a medium
         an agency of cultural mediation
welcome back to ice
watch thick time of transcorporeality
that nature / culture binary

provocative climate as meaning
                    gerund
multiscalar spatial frames for
the mundanity of literary criticism
            it's *so thick*
across the openings of deep time
                        weather time not strictly linear
            close to specific texts
Daphne's weathered substance the
quirks of that grammatical ambivalence
that southerly wind deified in Hesiod
                                            dipped in aspic
the spondee-an english; the anapestic greeks
            there he is
to be marble   relieved
of the weather in weathered texts
carried beyond   their georgic neighbourhood
weather is all—hostile wind
the blood of love corroding
            don anthropon
opportunistic weather in plato's *gorgias*
folding the lyric present against
            the dot-dot-dots
intransitive and weathered [derogatory]
into
~*Zoom*~ bodymind in weather
                                    oops
ovid the predatory male poet and
metaphors for ecological mesh
                    in gold notes
in the respiratory mingling of air with bodily
tissues
            you've become my *barometer*
her body both crumbly

rhymed in mingling
                    climate change   [pregnant pause]
lyric in its blue jeans
the weather: the code spoken by the moment
the phenomenology of the haiku
projective   verse
            kinesis of words & weather
he will have some several causations
she, Daphne, will have little / instant poems
the tyranny of the seed crystal insulator
        my microscope objective
ebullient & syntactically fecund
a very medium coincidence
            responsive to the weather as it is to
us
before the advent of the neurotic Anthropocene
of the weather   of the time
the diachronic nature of climate change is as such
                    inimical to historicism
"it's real. it's mythic. it's wild
        in the form of fallen snow
        as it is of a living
                    shaped by a mutability across
deep time
for poetry does indeed matter
        not a way of happening
        nil by mouth but
            why *ranches?*
what of weathering the storm? of betraying betrayal
put up with by racialised bodies
        rematerializing the metaphor of climate
        change and why you
shouldn't
        poets are always squeezing things

she's bound to find liquid squashed
between her pages a kind
        of hubris
hubris to think you could stand off from
the burning decay

                        i'm annoyed by the lyric south wind
                        poetry makes nothing happen except
                                piss me the fuck off

and anyway water is blank

the range of the awful hand is
nothing like the frisson of impending surgery
eloquence connotes proficiency connotes officiousness while
elegance connotes *grandeur*
dizzy says that *The Vestiges of Natural Creation* will be a great success
saunas heated by goodwill generated out of bitcoin mining
in territories where fully grown men should be clean shaven
there is a picture of a bee in this issue
               what do i look like
radicalised anyway? etymologies for the
petrodollar sink into recesses i never knew i had in me
       with just a software update
the tesla cybertruck is trying, trying
to ruin my evening and possibly even my ring finger
       A couple
       making love everywhere.
what a way to start this particular localised
slay
           whoever abuses his right to hospitality has forfeited his right to
             hospitality
or so you think but i've never
eaten better than on the pickets never
slept better than in the encampment
and still the assaulted body grows weaker and weaker
         would like to die telling a joke
              and died when the soul was wrenched out but
looney tunes style so don't cry *much*
between my finger and my thumb
the squat chip rests
              Gott im Himmel shedding speech: let him *cook*
for if it isn't the bigman! o honourèd serpent god then

i'm on my uppers and you are
the peeler going for his gun eternally
                    their ideological twins the ayatollahs in iran
the intelligence must resist the poem
                    may thy
                    riot gear
          chip and
                    shatter
                              hurting in the *air quotes*
the generative predicament of his entire hulking oeuvre
resist.   *next*
to dislike quotidian illness because it's uncomfortable well i'm built
     different
a horror of thoughts like the parliament of foules
the basket of lime already there
the killing we must cease
out of the (parenthetical), like Gertrude stein says, and into the recursive,
                    the recursive
               pondering the psychology of sweet nothings
                         out here on the gauzy frontier
                              between my finger
                              and my thumb

i'll dab with it

the good-for-nothing junior brother is
burning with desire and can't help
bossbaby
up thy ladder and
down thy vanity thy
infernal dreamies
at the conference on deodorant ethics
i played the elevator game and preferred
the other world
edging the city
young ones dabbing in the
cyclamen
send rudy   no jude
i have incense to clear you
where tradition meets incision
at makeout archipelago
due to the
unfortunate!
we are deeply out of
      onions
thx for understanding management
it's the heaney that gets you over the line
in debt ceiling deals:
that sweet spot where the mind
is at its most ululating
luminous
      full of
squat pluck
brother, everything is better than
lana del rey

rimming the metropolis
                    assess waterline ballast /
                    rejig of existing ballast
                    up the rigging
i tested out the time anomaly of the
Woolwich foot tunnel and preferred
it to the regular clockpunch
bush and the war on
vape:
reverse snobbery of the labouring
shoe-flinging classes
what do women do
            play better
when we're together
have your good time
aqueous
here's the list of folks *not*
invited to my barbecue sleepover
have to water her
trump lawn everyday
pity paunch thy XL pully brooch
rile the skinflint Wokerati
one wishes one's poems to be as
one's sturdy tribe

                                        limpid
                            carceral
                    penitent
            impotent
        and
so weak in this need for you

consign that to the
sillybilly quadrant of
brain under fire
file that under
girldinner
cookie crisp dogfood for boys
if that's postpostfeminism now then
call me girlbossboss
the need for a proliferated
deviancy of girlhood
(mutual and general assent)
oyez oyez
listen to women but also to me festival
some excoriating
littlemix
asocial pottery
catty-corner
creation studios
paternoster deathgrip
asocial Beyblade betting
racket
shortlist of 2: the pauls
who would be
forever young
i was the first responder on scene
at the sycamore gap massacre
the firebrand of the wicklow mountains
neither my method nor objective is poetry but
rather products:
fungible vibes, merchant aura
little ropes to pull you to the other, more fun side
once i've got one leg over i'll
write my lake isle

whore my skinsuit instead of donating it
in meagre little strips
that shropshire lad? why
he is my shropshire son
the eulogies tending funnier the further
from the event
blap
is hell making a comeback?
they call this huckstering do they and
that updoc?

they call these withdrawal symptoms the
DTs
(the donald trumps)
well colour me riddled
who had van gogh x Pokémon
collab
on their apocalypse bingo ticket
raclette
for ever
you love her but
you wouldn't read her
out
split my chaps on the infinity discourse
        and my lip on the flinty sickle
caught the eye of the security guard at
the own-the-libs AI light show
me, i dug the portmarnock
beach hole
blew the interview
botched my icebucketchallenge
squandered my necknomination
but see here
                Kunst ist schön
an english gentlewoman splits the G

RETURN ON INVESTMENT

i. teachta

one week into the RURAL HOURS i find
there isn't any light behind your delicate glass
eye you're growing weary of this *we* that wont
the sunbear brimming with confidence sipping
energy drink with most unnatural conclaves
   yon
      fusty clavicle
this is a tale for 4 year olds so stand down
your valiant woke troops there is no credulity left in my
powerful toddler son
one last feed of pints before mooring at
ringsend with cromwell and his bossom friends
cabbageheads in tow
everyone, young and old, is standing around
   eating crisps

ii. pionós

the blight is but an angry god
the rain is but a crying god
my maximalist lifestyle is but a blight on my
longsuffering loved ones who are altogether
   hungry
the ol' bob and wheel
and sleet is godpiss muzzled godspit
when a carved curve across the nightsky reads
     máthair
crudely

this is the way; step inside
this is the breadcrumb trail of deathstench
and dogshitbin
this puts hairs on chests
     the concept in concept album
     the rock in rock opera
the more narrative the further from internet
signal on the greened horizon flashes
f u c k f i n e g a e l f u c k f i a n n a f á i l
in morse like the eyelids of
the Vietnam war prisoner who hasn't yet realised
it's him who's the eternal tout
get out of my country   get out of my life and DMs
i hate your beefheart so much that
if black '47 had been my responsibility there'd have been
a pioneering tax credit
spreadable provided you possessed the requisite croppy pike
  or crozier
when jigs and reels bore even the dozer happy
without bed and board for the night
               have we become even *that* racist
get out of my country get out of my loved one's
hospital room with that twentyfirst century
language of english appeasement i have in my hand
a piece of shit

iii. naomhthacht

the sanctity of the wrong answer
the sanctity of thin gruel
the sanctity of emaciation of emigration
evisceration delirium tremens

cromwell's famous catchphrase:

paddy gives me the vertiginous ick

what would they have done to him in the flats
cromwell
      bald and beerbellied
domiciled in hostile benidorm
hulk hogan accidental lookalike
imported carling
        to hell or to hacienda
the only good taig is a taig mildly perturbed
the emergency is the great hunger is the munich bother is the
   ploughing is the poor mouth is
the definite article small matter
thank god they did not starve the forebears of
our latest and most effective capitalist
      mattress mick

iv. am caillte

to go away and come back hither for the sake of
seeing elaborate boat museums devoted to the gore and
striated bowels that were their eyes
your raisin d'être my flinty hearts to melt down sectarian peacelines
unzip faith reveal other similar faith
    sans prosecco
where you expected to find what politizians
call *hope*
     weren't we fucking tired before we were ever even
hungry?

v. éigeandála

tír gan teanga tír gan anam
tír gan bia tír gan tír
   gan béal
when hunger didn't put the doom in doom folk
we can't remember the hunger but we can
remember when the chickenfilletroll first
breached the 4 euro mark irreversibly
like a whale or a particularly ornery baby when
    jeans and sheux Trevelyan
   cryptosporidiosis
mica scandal
shackled penurious cancer
patients to a social duty to pay their
exorbitant rents
a line of flaming tents like it's effective to
burn a fucking tent
god forbid we're ever hungry again
we haven't the stomach for the most paltry
messages anymore except in lipstick

vi. scannal

     do NOT give to UPS: irish corn
     to england where liberty is a department store
     and a fucking expensive one
her hungry troops clad in Canada goose & gold
bloodthirsty but not discerning about blood
to be so meek and mild and yet so profoundly on   the   bag
would you like me to be your cat?
would you care to maim me?
to run me over with the English Tea Bus
   upon the westway?

do i eat shit and die? very well then i eat shit
and die (the septic tank is large, it contains tiny mortal remains)

hold your hand out, naughty boy; i saw ya
        now, *on to the dream land*

QUOTH GOOD UNCLE MOUTH

cradled in doggèd carrion among the shrouds of trojan Ulster /

apt auguries of things to come
mist and mellow fruitiness i.e.
here's the life i've always longed for
       i will make it mine
Pal, put down that big straw sack
& fill your pail with this poem.
Maybe you could give
touching a try
          this whitsun
I would like the countess of Monrosier
to hear all about my perfect poem.

a knock at the door, a funereal ritual
constant danger safe
down the upper falls
return doubtful honour &
             recognition
Baby, I admit one little fuckup.
pleathered in slag cream and
waste expanse:
507 frog people; 100 years old
that screaming men call silence
to crashing bat populations
     Scope & Contents
1 letter of compleynte unto pite
they'd tell me i was dead if
i ever booked my appointment
for the protruding eye

the touch of the rossetti
MILK KING,
seek help from medical professionals trained
in mental health
        sticker phantom limb
        shifty rob
Kubernetes solemn nodecluster as
a critic first and a soulmate second
                this is the
       "camino taco"
       turn off commodity volatility alerts lest
    thou be a breeder of market ergonomics
this has been
   the list

LUCY HOLME

SEA LION WOMAN COMES ON LAND, SWIMS IN POOL AND
STEALS MAN'S CHAIR LANE

Today a man watches me swim, waves—says, *a couple of points,*
if I may—so I cock my head to one side and lift my goggles.
He says I'm good but that my knees don't lock, they bend instead.
My arms must slice the water *just so*; my ankles *should be doing the work.*
If I really want to be faster, I should make myself *much lighter.*
In the water, I am like the sea lion I saw on the YouTube short,
who climbs the steps to a hotel terrace, carved into a tiny cove,
conquers the rocky staircase at top speed, frazzled
from supine pirouettes, from chasing sardines all day long.
He flips into the pool and glides the length in one graceful arc,
soaking terracotta pots and tiles, supplants a tourist on his chair,
moving spectacles and papers and sun lotion bottles out of his way.
My new coach says I should crouch like a frog on the wall, leap
forward underwater until I reach the end of the red buoys.
He shakes his head, looks dismayed. I do not breathe correctly.
If I can't learn the correct technique, I'll sink like a stone.
I think of the joy of a swim when you long to clear your head,
of the sea lion's perfect bulk, the weightless ache of a Puglian resort,
his strength as he ascends without using the steps. Just like him,
my freckled blubber gleams under strip lights and tattered flags,
steam blowing from my flaring nostrils as I swim, both eyes wide
open. I could be a predator too. Chase jellyfish tissues and rays,

tuck in my fore flippers and clap my thighs, heels up, toes down.
Even though my body is turned away, I sense the man coming
again to offer me some more of his expertise. But like the sea lion,
I know best how to manoeuvre my sizeable body in water.
My eyes glow red at night. With my third eyelid, I watch him
take notes on my performance, while I disrupt the surface calm.

that you cannot seem to pass has a question on *tuffeau* and you are relieved. This, surely, you can answer. After all, you have been to a restaurant carved like a lime-lithograph, flagstones mouldering—a misshapen candle bulbous in wine-bottle glass, air yellow-creamy with soft age. It was there you popped clean apple bubbles on your tongue, sharp pips laced with muscovite and silk. What a vitreous palate you had back then. But in-depth knowledge of Touraine and its bryozoan soils deserts you. You forget its sloping hills, the colours of local horses, the ratchet screws on oak presses. Nor do you recall the names of major rivers and trickling tributaries, the absence, the occurrence, the frequency of its golden mists. Your head is empty of hectares, of terroir, facts slip through the free-draining soil and you spend too long, are recklessly languid—the weighting all wrong—as you picture its chalky loam and that week in the Loire, under loose folds of mist, in a room you couldn't warm. By day you toured the sodden vineyards as grey-rot blossomed underneath your skin. At night, spat out the tartrate crystals not captured by the waiter's muslin cloth, ate red-raw venison squares, more delicate with each morsel than with each other. Instead of answers, you see the *Chateau de Saumur* and each intricate hedge broderie, the dewed lengths of the maze, of the emerald *tapis* and the pie you could not pronounce—*pithiviers*—scribbled in black biro in the margins and you draw an apologetic face and imagine the examiner smiling sadly as he fails you yet again. You list more dishes in bullet point form—*Rilettes de tour, Rabelais's fouace* and want to tell him how you studied *Gargantua and Pantagruel* at school as he passes stiffly with his waxy examiner's gaze—so he might consider you clever; to write that when pairing *Andouilette* no grape can cut through its fatty walls no matter what a French sommelier says. But you have run out of space now and your fingers hurt, and they refuse to give you any more paper. And you think—why did no one ever say you were not a good match? Or that a rain-soaked Loire in April would be a terrible mistake? Why did they not warn you about the damp that would spread to the bedrock of your gut from afternoons spent on musty cellar tours and buying En-Primeur; of the sly bathroom ghosts and the mediocre sausage gastronomy that would lodge in your gullet, and you don't feel guilty for saying all this just because he is dead. You'll admit you could have been a better companion on that mini-break, at times a better wife, and that you always were an average student of wine. Far more skilled at drinking it, at getting lost in boxwood topiary, at playing a role and filtering the truth, than describing the fleeting taste of lost love.

SHARING A CIGARETTE ON WEST 47TH STREET
—*for Philip Seymour Hoffman*

The night we saw *Death of a Salesman*
we sat in our seats at the Ethel Barrymore
and I was shocked when people laughed
at bits that weren't funny. Big bellows
from their guts, huge guffaws. For Christ's
sake, I thought. This isn't a *comedy*.
Was he having any fun by then? Joking
with the cast between scenes, lapping up
the encores. Shouldering this tale of failure,
of loneliness. Did it stick when the curtain
fell? I liked him best as Scotty in *Boogie Nights*.
In a red shiny bomber, big old strawberry blonde
head. Liquid with lust and misbegotten hope.
I mean—who among us hasn't misread a signal?
We've all been Scotty once or twice, crying
in a sports car over some guy at a party.
I had hoped we might meet outside after
the last curtain call. Share a cigarette.
He'd tell me where to find the tastiest
Reuben sandwich in the city, I would tell him
how much I enjoyed *The Ides of March*.
Running his hands through his hair he'd say
this is the classic american fable,
I'd better not fuck it up. I'd laugh and say
Philip! You were the perfect Willy Loman.
There's always a reason why men
want more than they have, he might say
(almost as an afterthought).

(YOU WERE) DECLUTTERING BEFORE MARIE KONDO MADE IT FAMOUS

Was it you who first told me Buddhists don't crave material belongings? You probably learned it from that book you thought was about seagulls but which turned out to be about higher living. I used to cling to mementos but I've hardened since our goodbye on the harbour wall, half-deafened by the birds' rancour as the *pescherecchi* emptied their nets, three bulging plastic bags pooling at your feet. Things never went as planned for you. Fired twice from jobs you didn't like, you escaped—or jumped—before you were pushed. This time it was personal. Our winter in Italy was supposed to be about drinking *affogato* and smoking on balconies at night, not deciding what to keep and what is worth losing. The Polaroids and cheap plastic mascots, those flea market pendants, gilt peeling to reveal a hard interior, all your good intentions re-apportioned. You didn't cry. Maybe you knew long before we did that you can't trust a single thing that doesn't breathe or talk back; that wealth like this can be poisonous if you inhale it long enough. Maybe you knew that by asking you to leave they would save your life. Back then you were so unruly, so ungovernable. They couldn't crack you like a crayfish, spears digging at your soft tissue, any more than I could have quit with you in solidarity. I tossed the Sperry Topsiders you had refused to wear, preferring to feel the cool teak under your feet, and the only way to demonstrate my love was to fold your old t-shirts at the shoulders the way you liked. You were opaque and the artefacts you discarded cast the faintest shadows. I checked your bunk for hair-ties and found that worn leather diary you bought the summer we docked in Split. I never read it. It was as if each charity shop bin bag I knotted, each pair of socks I balled were your discarded selves. I didn't want to understand you or to uncover the truth and while I am still enmeshed and unwilling to hollow out the past, I'll never ask.

LYNCHPIN AS FRAGMENT OF IMAGINATION.

lynchpin as silicone jelly mould of us / almost impossible to quieten and still

something more slippery / like a goldfish in a bowl you just can't catch /

ambiguous / somehow frightening / outside the realm of your tightest control

concrete as fabrication / made of tears / unnerving as a science experiment

without its initial hypothesis / lynchpin spending a very happy summer

in thrall to a friendship that never served you / when love both disarms

and resists sanctions / when you can't admit it's been your life-long pattern

locking on to one inappropriate person / after another / the confidence

of a lynchpin / what did Montaigne say again? / *because it was him /*
because it was me?

was there really no one else it could have been? / what if you needed

a stranger to dig you out / like a bronze-age pin? / to help you see the
implausibility

of your condition / to disrupt your stability / what if that was their function?

which is not to say that it was a wholly transactional kind of arrangement /
rather

that it was never solid / and always inevitable that you should break apart.

THE GARDENER
—after Joan Miró

I recreate the sky anew each night, gather it in my arms
like chestnuts at castanyades. The scene moves at the speed
of a promise, sudden as breath intake. I fear
I might tell every secret I have ever heard, just to fill
this silence. Stillness distorts; then, a gear change.
I need a new word for the time between now and dawn.
Our fair skin blisters in the day, irises bleached by the glare
of the sun's rapt attention. But tonight, I am a bale of hay
smoldering in the grove. I count the choristers
as they join the ensemble. Four separate avian calls
and a ringing chirp. One solitary, deep and husky bark.
A high-pitched jagged laugh and a speeding car.
Glass clink is a hurried *brindis*, the horizon shattered,
sharp yet mellow. A mewl like the fresh cry of a newborn.
At cockerel crow, a stray wolf howls, waiting for nightfall.
A constant *coo coooo coo*, a yappy bark, more urgent now.
Clap clap clap—I do not care to know that creature,
in whatever form it takes. A throatier growl, shrill scream.
Still the twitter and squeak of the unseen. Behind clouds,
the rough-hewn orange sun ducks down, last few rays diluted.
A plane strikes through the sunset. The wood pigeon sleeps.
I list the things I still recognise; there is so much I do not.
Little moon, distant dog, toad croak, dirt on my hands
and lining my pockets, *calima* that dyes your clothes red
and makes rivulets on the white tiles of a swimming pool.
And every few minutes—hot metal slices through sky
like a brusque but not unexpected warning. When I look
up again it is the bisque ombra of a half-forgotten
conversation. What were our last words? Miró once said
I want everything that I leave behind to stay just as it is
when I am gone.

REASONS TO BID ON A LIMITED EDITION *MANOLO BLAHNIK*
SHOEHORN ON EBAY AT 3 A.M.

Because I missed the vertiginous inanity, the pointless aluminium of it.
And because when I recall our losses it always leads me back to duplicity.
Because he never cared for us maudlin, singing to songs he did not know.

Because you always found the best, most thoughtful gifts and even now
in a senior executive role—and as a mother of two—you buy and wrap
all your Christmas gifts in June. But because I never learned to take care,

I got so drunk and mislaid the hologram bag you tied with a golden bow.
Because I went to Mahiki after dinner, guzzling *Heming-feis* in tiki cups
til late sparring with him in a fog of frosted glass and cocktail umbrellas.

Because I should have paid my share and gone home when you did.
Because I despised his pretensions and his constant un-asked for opinions
but couldn't tell you this because you believed he was the one.

Because I couldn't keep anything back then—my resolve, my word,
my marriage vows; principles lost to a VIP booth and the late night void.
Because we waved you off at Euston and he said *one more for the road—*

but he would never stop; even with blistered heels, even with trench foot.
Because I stayed out drinking, only to wake at 7 a.m. bathed in curtain
less white light, regret suffocating me like a 13-tog duvet in summer.

Because you called me later that day and I admitted to losing the presents,
but couldn't explain how. And, because, instead of being cross you sided
with me. *Don't feel bad*, you said, *you'll never beat him. You shouldn't even try.*

Because I haven't seen him since we stood on different sides of the town.
And because of the difference between being carefree and being careless.
Because no one knew what to say that morning, so they didn't make a sound.

Because your dress hung unworn in the bay window of that Amalfi hotel.
A 1950s dream, spotlessly white. I still see you unzipping the garment bag.
Because I never told him you were worth a million versions of him.

Because I could not stay in my unhappy marriage for the two of you.
Because he was the first great love of your life and I was jealous.
Because I need a reason to still hate him, though ten years have gone by.

Because you—thin as a needle by July—stitched yourself together again.
Because, when you chose *Cavalleria Rusticana* as your wedding song, I saw
Don Corleone falling out of his wicker chair, dead in the morning sun.

Because there should be good reasons why we forfeit the things we love,
but sometimes there are none. Because in the novel the Godfather's last words
were *life is so beautiful*. Because in the end, I lose the bid for the shoehorn.

DILLON JAXX

GODFISH †

i wait for the body of christ to dissolve † until a wet gob
slides from my milk tooth cage † i swallow and imagine
him swimming in my belly † the gaping godfish † held
within my plastic body † a prize i am not allowed to enjoy
a prize to be covered † coveted † consumed † but not by me
i realise i couldn't be eating him whole every week † i must
be eating bits † a finely sliced knee or knuckle bone †
a once fleshy organ dried and pressed into a white coin †
filling me like a piggy bank each Sunday † saving myself
for a rainy day † my hands need to stay palmed to each
other † not even allowed to reach in and pull him out †
i have felt heaven though † when her fist opened inside
me † held me until the sun rose and burnt our wings †
until the sun rose and the prayers our tongues had been
folded into slipped back down our throats genuflecting
to god's blind spot † rising in each other † prising hymns
from lips that had been until that very second sealed †
a school of goldfish is a troubling † a school of godfish
is a never-ending lesson to be mindful of what lives inside you

DISTENDED FAMILY

the coin operated telescope snatches
tenpence from my fingers /eager to give
up a glimpse of infinite horizons / there
in the middle of a salt and vinegar
ocean are the aunts / gabbling
on a flaccid lilo / making sandwiches
for boxing day / there is an orange
squash breeze / undertones of honey
puffs in a tumultuous sea / occasionally
on a lithium tide / the lilo topped with aunts
is cast ashore / they grab my hands / run
to the nearest church and roly-poly
down the aisle / we eat ice cream and lick
the ends of batteries to check how much
of life is left / the uncles are chippies /
our names carved into anything we want
made of wood / my cousins watch
with biscuit eyes / layers of family circle
and always at least one that's left
behind / back home Christmas lights
are only ever white / we have to stand
around the tree and think of Jesus /
but all i see is a handmade crucifix / the aunts
complete with lilo pinned against it /
the congregation mumbling prayers
as though they are ingredients for a meal
in a language they never plan to serve

TRANSUBSTANTIATION

this particular Sunday   lined up as usual
hands cupped one inside the other or tongues
out the less inhibited stand open
mouthed to receive a limb of god

when they announce that there is nothing
left today   we have eaten god in his entirety
and each of us are asked to give up
a part of ourselves to create

a new god   i run to the front bunching
my long hair in my fists   they lay me out
arrange my tangled shock behind me
hang it over the marble edge

of the altar and with one slice of the cleaver
cut me free   frankincense clouds waft
from metal kettles swung by altar boys
as we are given our new god's blessing

and permission to leave   i am first at the vast
carved doors running into my new life
hoping that whoever's eyes god has can see
me but whoever's hands he has can't reach

THE BODIES IN THE FRIDGES AT WORK

I suppose mortuary workers too might remember
a random event from two years ago and smile

as they cut open this chest. And when they break
for lunch, they might place slices of ham between

two slabs of bread and puzzle over a crossword
and the answers to none of the clues will be

the names on the tags attached to the toes
of the bodies in the fridges at work. And I suppose

mortuary workers might plant bulbs and watch buds
birth through the dirt from underneath. And, when

they open the fridge and the light shines onto the last
hardening third of cheese, it will not remind them

of the bodies in the fridges at work. Someone must
make a living colouring in grey lips once plump

and dripping with gossip and mama's best homemade
ragout. I could not be a mortuary worker surrounded

by flesh. And yet, every night at dinner, whether a
quick sandwich or a laboriously constructed lasagne,

making sauce the way he taught me, salad on the
side, I eat surrounded by dead people. My brother's

beautiful, bruised cadaver at the head of the table.

PULCINELLA

my Italian grandfather was tailor
                    my English grandad was a circus
                              clown   from the two sets of genes
    my brother
class comedian   affable jokesmith who liked
                              to have everyone in stitches
he inherited Punch and an incomplete magic set
                              practised early the art of disappearing
things   my heirloom was a mending kit   i never got to use
                              long since lost
                                        in one of many moves but Punch
is in my kitchen   the wooden-headed puppet
                              a too wide grin cut
            into his timbered face   a claret
                              gown to hide the puppet
                              master's hand   the tang
            of pocket money silver and ropes cling
                                                  to his hem
i've bagged him like a piece of evidence   fearful
                    that if i let him out he'll come alive   turn
                              into a real boy or worse a man and pull me
            into his nightmares   disguise
                              it as a show
            and still i can't let go   i keep the creature
                              close and dream
                                        of conjurers
                    of needles in hot spoons
                                        of magic tricks
        of ligatures and limbs   my brother laughing

                    reappearing any moment now

KLEMENTINENLACHKRAMPF*

is what they called it this   fit
of giggles they fell into as
they boarded the Arlberg
express in Innsbruck because
they   had   been   eating
clementines   an   icy   dusk
pulling   their   train   toward
Christmas

Dad   paid   for   the   entire
couchette so nobody could
intrude   to   claim   the
unoccupied bed the boy is
ten   at most eleven the girl
six   at   most   seven   that's
the story   there's no three-
act structure here   no wordy
amble   to   a   brutal climax
no surprise tucked away in
between the railway lines

this is the destination   the
mouths of these children
fizzing with giggles zesty
breaths   maybe   some   pith
caught in a milk tooth fence
like a question   stay here
with me   in this moment
let's pull

this mouth around us   make
soft furnishings of warm
cheeks   hopscotch tongue
bask in citrus breath   these
children are now   no sense of
hours left to travel   or miles
the train will pull along tracks
in the dark   no sense of how
long their journey might be

how small this moment
blurred like landscape fleeing
outside the window this silly
snapshot   pitstop in a long
journey that is passing things
as we look back trying to
focus on something beautiful
before it's gone

*lit trans clementine giggles

MY BROTHER'S NEEDLEWORK

was heart stopping # in German #
the language we grew up with #
fixer means junkie # because whilst we sit
in judgement of dark shadows #
gathering like a plot # in the throat
of the underpass # they are trying
day after day to sew up the same old
wounds # and some # like my brother #
run # out # of # thread #

JAM KRAPRAYOON

WEATHER REPORT

A red warning was issued on Friday as a cloud of uncertainty blanketed most of the country. The weatherman's lip trembled at a low hum. He kept repeating, *we are all in desperate need of love*, tears streaming as the camera panned out slowly. Already you can observe its effects. Dates changed at random: my birthday three months late, Rome falls in 450AD or never at all. In the span of a few hours, my mother was spotted in a park in Brasilia, again in Agra and finally in a small diner in Texas. By Saturday morning, the fog was so dense we couldn't tell ourselves apart. I left my house and saw the streets, wider and emptier than before. The shelves were stripped bare of canned food, bottled water, toilet roll. All was gone but a lone trolley. Within, a half-eaten apple. Within that, a worm trembling at the core.

SCENES FROM THE UNDERWORLD
After Kiefer / After Joyce / After Homer

I   A man steps out of a funerary carriage. He takes a sword out and uses it to draw a circle on the ground. Into it, he pours libations for the dead: honeyed wine spiced with yarrow, and pure spring water. He offers up one young heifer, as large and black as the world. He carves her up and piles the flesh and bone high upon the altar before pushing it all into the boiling sea. He then calls the dead to him.

II   Half of the city has been levelled in the past hour. Buildings turned to rubble, frames of rebar warped into a close-knit tweed or like magnetic fields wrapping around a planet. A family orders take-out in a fast food joint on the outskirts of town and eats silently in the car. They have two large sodas, two cheeseburgers, and two fudge sundaes.

III   A woman heads to the bank to see if her mortgage is approved. She'll turn thirty-three in September, and most of her friends own homes already. The agent reaches across the desk and places his hand between her breasts. He pushes forcefully until her skin and sternum are punctured. Pulling out her heart, he places it on one end of a scale. On the other is a feather. She looks on, mind circling round and round, fingers moving fitfully.

IV   In April, a boy walks along the shore. The sand is grey ash, and the sea is snot green. A dog washed up dead on the beach. He pokes the body and stalks around it before falling still. He reaches into his schoolbag and takes out four chocolate coins wrapped in gold foil. He crouches down and places two in the dog's mouth. He unwraps the other two and eats them.

V   A man stands at the foot of a long staircase. He opens a wooden chest and summons the memory of his wife: she is thrusting a chunk of crushed seedcake into his mouth, following it with her full wet lips. It's their fifth anniversary. He closes the chest and sends off the priest. Walking up the stairs, his long blue robe stretches out behind him like the evening sky.

VI   A woman dreams her home is occupied by six plump geese from the river nearby. They eat all the wheat, but she is glad for the company. Suddenly, an eagle with a pointed beak swoops down from the mountain and breaks their necks, killing them. Awakening, she finds she has been crying, her tears watering the world over.

VII   In a library, students live under glowlamps, their minds impaled by golden serpents. Each book on the shelves is made of lead and inscribed with cryptic symbols. The students work hungrily and in pairs to turn the heavy pages. Each of the seven tomes promises knowledge: of the world, God, and their own dissolution.

∞   A janitor comes in to clean the office. Last night there was a party, so bottles and cups litter the desks and chairs are strewn about the floor. She bends over to pick up a toppled Christmas tree, still wrapped in shiny red garlands. She knows what she has to do. Yesterday's remains must be removed before 8 am sharp. Whistling to herself, she seems hopeful.

You're going into surgery soon. I imagine the scalpel, unravelling you into rain. I am meeting you for the first time again. Us, under the umbrella. Nervous-sharp and shivering. You show me your sketches. The subject— a woman in a kimono, decaying in the woods. Matter-of-factly, you explain how each panel shows a stage of death. I scan a bare shoulder, peeking out of her robes, and see you. Flush and grand and naked. But her body already shows signs of slack. She's alone in the open air. The bloating starts. Her belly, a gray and waxing moon. Swollen with hours, the skin splits and slips away. From below, everything is rising. Her stomach opens and collapses in. Not long after, the worms come. And then dogs and birds to pick at what's left. The sky behind, flat and perfect gray. Like our day out in Highgate, walking among the graves. You asked me to name the exact colour of the headstones, and I didn't know. All I knew was we were running late, but had no good reason to hurry.

AN INVENTORY OF INVASIVE SPECIES

Chestnut blight, which nearly wiped out the American Chestnut,
comes first as a breath, enters the wounds of trees and grows
in and beneath the bark, leaving arcs of dark buttered copper.

Cinnamon fungus, also known as *heart rot* or *ink disease,*
crumbles root tissue and chokes off a plant from water
its heartwood hollows out, its stems wilt and darken.

The *African tulip tree,* also called *flame of the forest*
for its fat clusters of florid bulbs, has a hot pollen
that brings a sudden, burning end to honey bees.

Soapbush, which is also known as *Kosters' curse*
after some locals falsely pinned its introduction
on a neighbouring sugar planter from abroad.

Fall webworms, which eat the tender leaves
but avoid the larger veins and midrib
shrouding their meal in a silken mist

just like when ortolans were eaten,
diners would cover their heads
under a white cloth napkin

to hide their bald shame
from God above
and *each other*.

SHORT EXCERPT FROM *THE COMPLETE BOOK OF FATE*

(Formerly in the possession of Napoleon, late emperor of France, and now first rendered into English, from a German translation, of an ancient Egyptian manuscript found near Mount Libycus, in upper Egypt.)

★ ★ ★ ★ ★
★ ★　　★

★ ★ ★ ★ ★　　Your life will take on a new hue. Perhaps a rich dale gold
★ ★　　　　or Prussian brown. It may even tend towards malachite.
　　　　　　You don't recognise it, but as you grope toward it, you
　　　　　　will find it is oddly shaped and liminal. It will have the
　　　　　　consistency of cuttlefish bone and the flavour of mummy
　　　　　　powder.

★ ★ ★ ★ ★　　You will visit a nearby gaming house. Ignore the dagger-
★　　　★　　stares of the croupier and his unsightly smoked-tinged
　　　　　　vest. Behold the despair of the gambler, who has just
　　　　　　lost his all— then play. Only put up what is precious to
　　　　　　you but that you are willing to part with. Don't expect to
　　　　　　regain what you've lost.

★ ★ ★ ★ ★　　At last, you will have unexpected success with a new
★　　　★　　diet. Floating at the bottom of the ocean, the sulfur-rich
　　　　　　volcanic ash will sustain you. The seeping heat of nearby
　　　　　　geothermal vents will keep you warm. You will outlive
　　　　　　us all.

★ ★ ★ ★ ★　A vast empire to the west will burst the bonds that fetter
★ ★　　　　it. The bolts will be drawn, the doors opened, and chains
broken. A colony of outcasts will come to power. Its
natural resources will make it an emporium of commerce
and art. Later, while the winds are still and the air calm,
the earth will quake suddenly, and those on its surface
will be swallowed up.

★ ★ ★ ★ ★　You will make a lifelong friend, though they will
★　　　　　　complicate rather than complete you. You will cast about
for a centre, questioning the engine of your life. But they
also mix a stiff sazerac, which you can appreciate.

★ ★ ★ ★ ★　Beware entering into the land of strangers. There they
★　　　　　　have built a great machine, though its mechanisms
are inscrutable. It brings both unbounded wealth and
unbounded peril. Those who use it may be transformed.
Some will come to worship that machine and attribute to
it magical powers. If you go off to that far country, you'll
never come home again.

★ ★ ★ ★ ★　A strange contagion will take you in the coming days. The
symptoms are as follows: nervous sweating, involuntary
shudders, an increased heart rate and reddening skin
below the eyes. Take care, or you will spread it to others.
This is a terminal case of love, and it will watch you go
down with the sun.

A chyron blares across a screen: *The House is not in order.* I'm in the Senate cafeteria, half-watching C-SPAN. Republicans nominate another Speaker. Striped ties and flag pins shuffle in and out the room. My colleague stabs at a plate of dry falafel. We're like children wearing suits.

*

Penny shares a video of someone crawling up the Vegas Sphere. He's climbed past a massive advert for a U2 concert. The city spreads out below him: the Vegas Strip glows like a burn pit in the desert, its fossil sounds buzz in the dark.

*

John Cena stands shirtless on top of the announcer's table. He tells the crowd that Bin Laden has been *compromised to a permanent end.* Roars of *USA USA USA* break out across the arena. Cena hands out high-fives. The sound guys cue *The Stars and Stripes Forever* as his hand rises to salute.

*

After September 11th, my family left our house near DC and stayed for a while with our friends, the Patels. I played Game Cube with the other kids, heard helicopters churning the sky above us. I couldn't tell then how scared they all were.

*

A Ukrainian watch collector buys a pair of golden *Never Surrender* sneakers for $9,000. Signed by Trump himself. *What I hate to see is division*, the collector says to a reporter. *We're one people under one flag.*

*

In Ms. Bryant's kindergarten class, I pledge allegiance for the first time. To the flag, the republic. I don't know all the words, but like how they rumble in my throat. Right hand squeezing my foreign heart. Stars and stripes in my eyes.

ESCHATOLOGY

I have spent the last fourteen hours
in the Times Square Margaritaville
drinking by myself, blankly staring
at a buzzing monitor. Images in motion:
rubble, weeping women, men
standing in uniform. I have killed
my appetite. The walls and floor
rearrange themselves. I help myself
to another fluorescent tiki drink
and watch a man walk into the bar
backwards. He doesn't seem to notice
the hole where his chest should be,
licks of cooling flame flicker off
his cratered body as he orders a drink
from the barman. The beer sloshes up
his gut and gullet, up out his mouth
and funnels neatly back into a bottle.
I look up and see rubble again.
They've announced an offensive now
or possibly a counteroffensive.
I check the clocks. It's a couple of minutes
to closing time. On TV, men in suits and ties
shake hands on stage, huddle close, clasp arms
to dance a final frantic can-can.
While we applaud, some grand firework
arcs through the air before it cracks
its yolk out and fills the sky,
a blossom of hot white-gold which rises
over the lined trees, the lights, the clouds
split by tall spires and begins
to lift everything away.

ADAM PANICHI

SNOW

Tool-rough palms guide his brother's foamy hand.
> *Get that bit under your chin.*
There over the bathroom sink
    he sees a million lives in his brother's
   eyes.
They're expressive now as his brother reaches out, trying to paint his nose
  white.
C'mon, don't be a silly bugger. He rinses the blade under the running tap
          holds it gently
           to taut skin.
Stand still now. One time, as he lay in bed
      with a girl she asked him his deepest secret. He
   lied.
His brother has given up asking
    what it's like to go with someone. He wishes he could have told him.
      There are still so many things he wishes he could
  understand.
He has never prayed for himself but every night
        he prays for his brother to get better.
He still picks the skin around his nails, probably will
   forever.

Mam'll have a fit if I nick you.
                        The razor moves as if peeling a film of air
                                        from a pressed flower.

                For the first time he sees his brother's face
            glistening, wet. A fresh patch of earth.

To look at it, you would believe anything could grow there.

When at a young age your body's boundary / desiccates / when folded sheet of mudcracked skin / you learn many big words / pruritic / atopic / lichenification /

Mother / ceremonious with her emollients / milky baths / occlusives / little-fingerfuls of hydrocortisone / would put me to bed oily / as a marine mammal feels /

It's an undefined border / topical steroid addiction / Biology kindling bushfires / across your dark country / you boiling to death from the inside / the only release / gouging thinning tissue / red streaks on bed sheets / badlands / engulfing backs of knees /

When paring fingernails failed / mother taped my hands in cotton gloves /

Imagine yourself bound / stinging nettle dangled / just near enough / to your eyelid / that a low breeze lets it peck / now remember / your impuissant / hands /

I still loathe this body under moonlight / would give up my nation in an instant / for gratification

CUPID, GROWN

In youth my leaf was smooth as a Ken doll's. I was Cupid then,
saw myself through a hand mirror. No one can other you
quite like yourself. In the hot keen night, I would fold the thing
between my legs into the neck of a swan asleep. The god of love emasc-
ulated; I tried to give myself to men. Men at my father's football club,
potent with Deep Heat's musk, swung fat cocks around the showers,
soaping them the way a warrior whets his blade.
Romans wore amulets of the phallic divine, dangled tintinnabula
in doorways, from horses when they rode in battle. I too have offered
a pinch of flour, hung one around my own neck, hoping.
But now I'm Eros, virile, god of desire—
playful in the mirror. I've untucked myself. Watch me
rattle my train of blisteringly coloured feathers.
I drink whiskey. I shave my chest. I put men on their knees.

BATHHOUSE

Steam rises, a question in the room:
wet, dripping and mingling with sweat.
It's hard to age a person from their genitals
alone, much less the way they yearn.
Somewhere in a darkroom, a man pulls
secrets out of another man. We men have long
held our motives for coming, this non-place
its organic edges, for meeting eyes as if through
an amoeba's membrane. The lamps are dimmed,
we all believe, to preserve fantasy; we fear light
will reveal how gently we touch ourselves.

TENDING

Eleonora Pucci snaps blue latex
over a wrist like a *badante*
readying her caregiving rite.

She scans his marble skin, attentive
to tiny fractures at ankles, counts webbed
fibres in sculpted locks of age-bleached hair.

Personal care is even more tender
than intercourse. I recall the clenched stitch,
tasked with washing a man older than my father,

expected gloved hands to waver,
ground beef strained in cheesecloth—
as he disrobed, I kept a towel between us

not, as I'd have thought, to guard my eyes
but in the way a mother bird furls her wing
around breakable young.

My hands bearing for the first time
his softened mass, were steadfast,
pure as bathwater.

Eleonora climbs a scaffold, taller
than three of her, to look into David's cordate
eyes, sets her gentle tools to task.

CARCIOFI

The year your mother cedes the kitchen
she gives me a bag of artichokes.
Picking one out, she warns me
to take care with the spines.
Her knife is blunt but familiar, her hands tire
opening up its stubborn head.
I take over. Your mother was raised on chestnuts
and things made of chestnuts or things
made from the flour of milled chestnuts.
È più quello che sprechi che quello che mangi,
she says, teaching me to test
when you've snapped away enough bracts
to find the tender middle. The last leaf
is always most sincere: yields
while holding form.
Your mother can still
fill a table to exhaustion. Amore,
I know it's hard seeing her this way.
Quick, while it's hot, let's eat. *A tavola.*

IN FRONT OF A ROTHKO YOU LEARN YOUR MOTHER HAS A SKIN TUMOUR

You ask sometimes what colour I see
when we're looking at paintings
or the sky together

a sort of guessing game,
an experiment you like to run. You laugh
when I miscolour them.

Che pazzesco, you say, *I'd love
to see with your eyes.*
My heart breaks, a null

hypothesis. It's divided
into two parallel planes, the canvas:
charcoal over light grey.

We take turns to rest
perched on one leg like water birds,
the other holding the sleeper up.

When did we start making pleas
to the grownups like *Please,
for me...* I daren't ask

what that makes us. After the long
time we move to another canvas,
I promise,

where I ask you to stare
at the central block of colour, hard
to look at like fresh yolk cracked

into a black day, until it hurts
until I'm certain
you see what I see.